THE LINCOLN ASSASSINATION

AT FORD'S THEATRE

Now He Belongs to the Ages

BECKON BOOKS

As we commemorate the 150th anniversary of Abraham Lincoln's assassination, we recall the indelible mark his leadership has left on history, and we celebrate his noble efforts to ensure our country's founding principles would be enjoyed by all Americans.

The remarkable collection of objects featured in this book brings us closer to Lincoln on that tragic night — the spectacles and linen handkerchief in his pocket, the top hat and great coat he was wearing. It is through this unique collection of everyday items that we are reminded of the ability of one individual to change the course of history.

On behalf of all employees of United Technologies, we are proud to partner with Ford's Theatre Society in presenting the *Ford's 150* commemoration events.

— Gregory J. Hayes, President and Chief Executive Officer, United Technologies Corporation

FORD'S THEATRE
Today Ford's Theatre is a working theatre, historical monument, museum and learning center that welcomes thousands of visitors each year.

April 2015 marked the 150th anniversary of Abraham Lincoln's assassination. We at Ford's Theatre are humbled and awed by the power of this man 150 years later and the impact of his life and legacy — not only on our country but also on the world.

This book explores artifacts from the unparalleled collection regularly featured at the Ford's Theatre campus, as well as a selection of other exceptional items related to the assassination from institutions across the country. In 2015 these rare items were reunited at Ford's Theatre for the first time since 1865 to mark the anniversary of Lincoln's death.

Through these artifacts, we gain insight into the very human figures at the center of the Lincoln assassination — figures who can often seem mythic and inscrutable.

We see Lincoln the man in the contents of his pocket from the night of the assassination: everyday items like spectacles, a pocketknife, a watch fob and a handkerchief. It was fascinating to learn that Lincoln carried a $5 Confederate note that night — perhaps it was a souvenir to remind him the war was ending?

We also see the impact on those close to the assassination in the eyewitness account of Dr. Charles Leale, who — only six weeks out of medical school — was the first doctor to aid the president. His letter details how he orchestrated Lincoln's care throughout the long night.

And in the playbill from *Our American Cousin*, we are reminded that, for its patrons that night, Ford's Theatre was not the site of a national tragedy, but a place where people gathered for respite and entertainment. The performance on April 14, 1865, was a highly anticipated event, a chance to relax and rejoice at the end of the war. The lives of those in attendance, however, would never be the same.

Through this book and the collection of artifacts it features, I hope you will gain a new understanding of this singular transformative moment in American history, as well as rediscover the American president against whom all others are measured.

— PAUL R. TETREAULT, Director, Ford's Theatre Society

HIS FINAL JOURNEY
The Center for Education and Leadership at Ford's Theatre highlights Lincoln's presidency and assassination. A fourth floor exhibit (pictured) re-creates Lincoln's funeral train.

WAR'S EFFECT
When this 1863 photograph was taken, two years of war with thousands of deaths and endless worry had left their mark on Lincoln's features.

"O shades of night — O moody, tearful night!" — WALT WHITMAN

April 14, 1865, was one of the happiest days of Abraham Lincoln's life. Since Lee's surrender on April 9, Lincoln had been more buoyant than at any other time during his presidency. During a carriage ride with his wife on the afternoon of the 14th, he said, "Mary, I consider *this* day, the war has come to a close. We must both be more cheerful in the future. Between the war and the loss of our darling Willie we have both been very miserable." Freed from the vexations of war and death — he would no longer have to send armies of young men to die — Lincoln dreamed of the future. Yes, he and Mary would be happy again.

What happened next changed the course of American history: Abraham Lincoln's triumphant arrival at Ford's Theatre; a single gunshot; the exultant cry of "Sic semper tyrannis"; the escape of the assassin; and the long vigil from midnight to dawn for the mortally wounded Lincoln. We have replayed that fateful night in our collective memory for a century and a half, but we can never change the ending.

The news stunned the nation. In the words of one reporter, "A stroke from Heaven laying the whole of the city in instant ruins could not have startled us as did word from Ford's Theatre a half hour ago that the President had been shot." At the supreme moment of victory, Abraham Lincoln had been assassinated. The mood of the nation changed overnight from inexpressible joy to unimaginable grief. "A nation bendeth down in tears," said one account.

One million Americans viewed his corpse when it was placed on public view in the great cities of the North, and 7 million people watched his funeral train pass by as it chugged westward, carrying Lincoln home to the Illinois prairie. Walt Whitman immortalized that journey in his poem "When Lilacs Last in the Dooryard Bloom'd."

> *Coffin that passes through lanes and streets, ...*
> *With the tolling, tolling bells' perpetual clang,*
> *Here, coffin that slowly passes,*
> *I give you my sprig of lilac.*

Clanging bells, black bunting and crepe and fragrant flowers — these were the sounds, symbols and scents of the spring of 1865.

It is altogether fitting that Ford's Theatre should commemorate the 150th anniversary of the death of Abraham Lincoln. It was on Tenth Street, in the nation's capital, that the great tragedy unfolded at Ford's Theatre and the Petersen House. And it was this tragedy that transformed Abraham Lincoln from a mortal man into America's secular saint.

This book brings together a selection of major artifacts from that "moody, tearful" and terrible night. The artifacts bring history alive in a vivid way that words alone cannot achieve. We hope that the following pages transport you back in time to Civil War America, when the death of one man after the deaths of so many caused a nation to weep.

In commemoration of the 150th anniversary of President Lincoln's passing, we present this book as our small token — our "sprig of lilac" — that we offer in memory of Father Abraham.

— JAMES L. SWANSON, Advisory Council, Ford's Theatre Society
Author, *Manhunt: The 12-Day Chase for Lincoln's Killer*

Abraham Lincoln

The nation's 16th president, Abraham Lincoln was born in rural Kentucky in 1809 and grew up primarily in Indiana. Mostly self-taught, he went on to become a post-master, militia captain, circuit lawyer and Illinois state representative. In 1842, he married Mary Ann Todd. They had four sons, though only the oldest, Robert, lived to adulthood. Lincoln served just one term in the U.S. Congress (1847–1849) before pursuing a career as a lawyer. His fiery debates with Democrat Stephen Douglas in 1858 earned Lincoln both acclaim in the antislavery Republican Party and a place on their presidential ticket in 1860. A moving orator and master politician, President Lincoln deftly guided the nation through its greatest struggle since the Revolutionary War. He was assassinated in Ford's Theatre on April 14, 1865.

America at Odds

On April 9, 1865, Confederate General Robert E. Lee surrendered to Union General Ulysses S. Grant in Appomattox Court House, Virginia. This marked the beginning of the end of the American Civil War. Those four years had been the bloodiest in the nation's history, with as many as 750,000 killed. President Lincoln urged Grant to extend mercy to Lee and his men, so when Lee asked for assistance for his hungry Confederate troops, Grant provided 25,000 rations of food and allowed the soldiers to keep their horses.

In Washington, the news of Lee's surrender was met with both jubilation and relief. Washingtonians illuminated buildings with candles and gaslights, and even serenaded the homes of their leaders.

While the North celebrated the Union victory, the South struggled with defeat. Much of the war had been fought in the Confederate states, a region that depended largely on agriculture for its survival. The war left the rail system in disrepair and farmlands in ruin. Compounding the issue, 4 million former slaves began to encounter a host of new obstacles and challenges in their difficult transition to freedom.

LEE'S SURRENDER
When General Robert E. Lee surrendered to General Ulysses S. Grant in April 1865, some Confederate forces were still fighting in the field. The North would not declare a final victory until June.

On the evening of April 11, Lincoln spoke from the White House balcony, where a jubilant crowd had gathered and started chanting his name. Reporter Noah Brooks held a light so the president could read, and Lincoln's youngest son, Tad, gathered his father's pages as they fluttered to the floor. In his speech, Lincoln hinted at his plans for the postwar South, highlighting his desire to provide suffrage to some formerly enslaved men. "It is … unsatisfactory to some that the elective franchise is not given to the colored man," he stated. "I would myself prefer that it were now conferred on the very intelligent, and on those who serve our cause as soldiers."

In the crowd that night was actor John Wilkes Booth. Booth sympathized with the South and vigorously supported the Confederate cause. As Lincoln gave his endorsement of African-American suffrage, the famous actor allegedly exclaimed, "That's the last speech he'll ever make."

JOHN WILKES BOOTH
While performing *The Marble Heart* at Ford's Theatre in 1863, Booth directed some of the play's most threatening lines at the president, who was in attendance.

GLORIOUS NEWS
The April 14, 1865, issue of the Pennsylvania *Bedford Inquirer* trumpeted the end of the war, stating, "God has granted victory!"

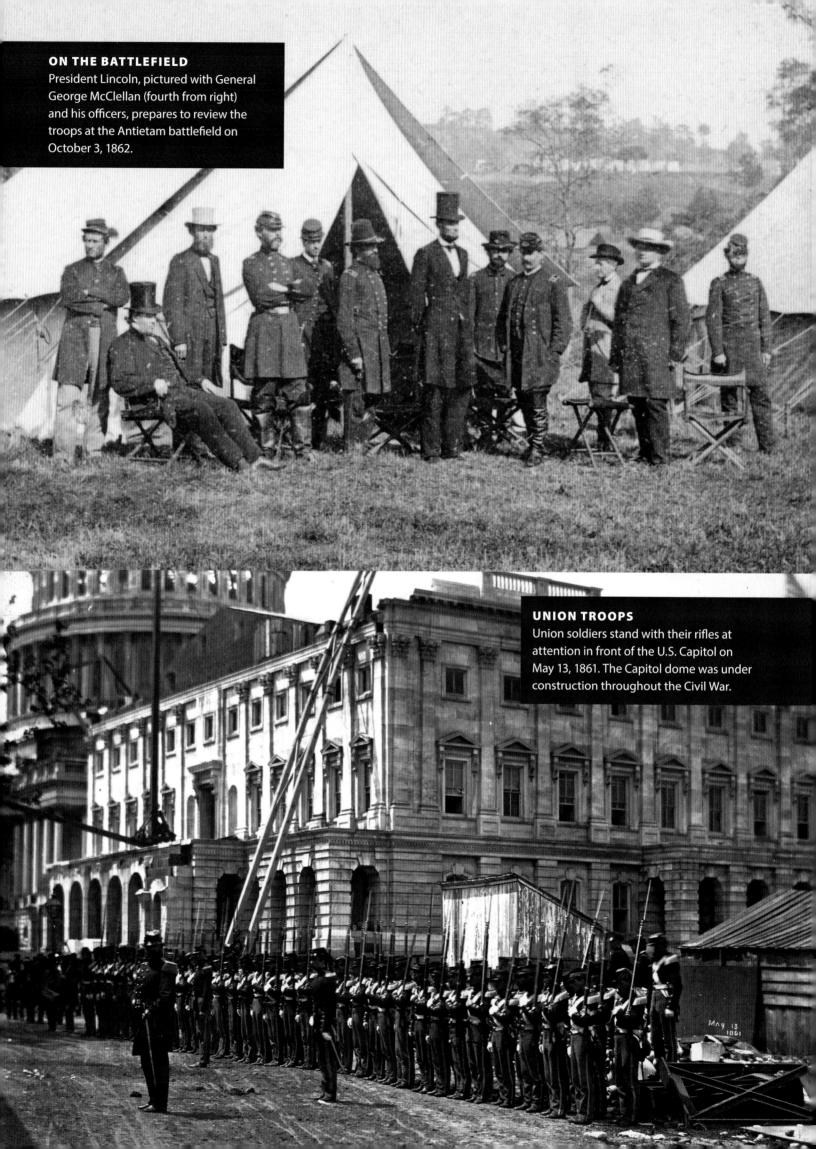

ON THE BATTLEFIELD
President Lincoln, pictured with General George McClellan (fourth from right) and his officers, prepares to review the troops at the Antietam battlefield on October 3, 1862.

UNION TROOPS
Union soldiers stand with their rifles at attention in front of the U.S. Capitol on May 13, 1861. The Capitol dome was under construction throughout the Civil War.

Lincoln's Top Hat

Harry Rubenstein, National Museum of American History

At 6 feet, 4 inches tall, Lincoln towered over most of his contemporaries. He chose to stand out even more by regularly wearing high top hats. Lincoln bought this silk hat from J. Y. Davis, a Washington hatmaker whose label appears inside the crown. The hat, approximately a modern size 7⅛, is trimmed with two bands: a thin ⅜-inch ribbon with a small metal buckle and a 3-inch grosgrain black mourning band that has discolored over time. The wide band signaled Lincoln's ongoing mourning for his son Willie, who died of typhoid fever in 1862. In a very public way, Lincoln was linking his own loss with the losses of so many during the war.

We do not know when Lincoln purchased the hat or how often he wore it. We do know that the last time he put it on was to go to Ford's Theatre on April 14, 1865. The War Department recovered the hat from the Presidential Box shortly after Lincoln's assassination and added it to the evidence used in the trial of the conspirators. Once the trial concluded, the hat was transferred to the Interior Department to be safely stored with other national relics that the department maintained at the Patent Office.

In 1867 the Patent Office sent the hat to the Smithsonian Institution. Secretary Joseph Henry, who had served as one of Lincoln's science advisors, ordered the hat to be immediately stored and placed in the basement of the Smithsonian. He cautioned the staff "not to mention the matter to any one, on account of there being so much excitement at the time." Although Henry did not further explain his decision, it appears he believed that displaying an item so closely associated with Lincoln's assassination was offensive and that pandering to curiosity seekers would only disrupt the institution's important scientific work.

The hat remained in storage and would not be seen by the public until the Smithsonian lent the hat to a Washington, D.C., gallery in 1893. Once the hat was made public, the Smithsonian Institution recognized that the artifact, which was so much a part of Lincoln's persona, was one of its greatest treasures.

The top hat that President Lincoln wore on the night of April 14, 1865, was silent witness to a perfect moment in time — a brief, happy interlude that was shattered by the brazen assassination. The president was at peace, looking forward to stepping away from the burdens of war. In an instant, his joy and the nation's hope were dashed, and horror, anxiety and sadness filled the theatre, emotions that would soon reverberate throughout the nation.

— EDNA GREENE MEDFORD, Professor of History, Howard University
Author, *Lincoln and Emancipation*

The Conspiracy

John Wilkes Booth's conspiracy developed over many months and involved several collaborators. As early as the summer of 1864, Booth met with Confederate agents to discuss taking Abraham Lincoln hostage and using him as ransom in exchange for the freeing of rebel prisoners. With the help of his childhood friends and Confederate Army veterans Samuel Arnold and Michael O'Laughlen, Booth planned to kidnap Lincoln while the president traveled between the White House and his summer cottage on the grounds of the Soldiers' Home.

As his kidnapping plan came together, Booth brought more Confederate sympathizers into the plot. John Surratt — a Confederate courier with extensive knowledge of the roads between Washington and Richmond and contacts in the Confederate government — was an early recruit. His mother, Mary Surratt, ran a boardinghouse near the corner of Sixth and H Streets, less than a mile from the White House — a convenient meeting place for the conspirators. Lewis Powell, a former Confederate soldier, and George Atzerodt, a Prussian immigrant, were occasional boarders at Mary Surratt's house. The final addition to the group was David Herold, an acquaintance of John Surratt.

In the wake of Lee's surrender to Grant, Booth's plans began to change. He realized that abducting the president would no longer help negotiate a Confederate victory. Disappointed but determined, Booth continued to dedicate his energies to the conspiracy.

On the morning of April 14, Booth learned that Lincoln would be attending Ford's Theatre that night, and he saw an opportunity to put his plan into action. Instead of kidnapping the president, however, Booth would kill him. This seemed like the only option, with just one day to plan and only half his co-conspirators available to assist. John Surratt was in Canada on a mission authorized by Confederate Secretary of State Judah P. Benjamin, and Arnold and O'Laughlen had left Washington.

ATZERODT'S KNIFE
George Atzerodt was assigned to kill Vice President Johnson. His knife was later retrieved and used as evidence in his trial.

The remaining men — Atzerodt, Herold and Powell — agreed to help Booth arrange the details of the new plot. It would be a simultaneous, three-part strike: on the president at Ford's, on Secretary of State William Seward at his home across from the White House and on Vice President Andrew Johnson in his hotel room on Pennsylvania Avenue.

GEORGE ATZERODT
Atzerodt immigrated from Prussia at the age of 8. He ferried Confederate spies across the Potomac River during the war.

DAVID HEROLD
As a pharmacist's assistant, the 23-year-old Herold had access to chemicals that were valuable to Booth.

LEWIS POWELL
Powell left the Confederate Army in January 1865, swearing an oath of allegiance to the Union under a false last name — Paine.

John Wilkes Booth

As a member of America's most celebrated theatrical family, 26-year-old John Wilkes Booth was noted for his good looks and athleticism on stage. Although Booth was familiar to Washington audiences for his performances in *Richard III* and other Shakespearean tragedies, he never quite matched the critical acclaim garnered by his father, Junius, and brother Edwin, who were among the foremost actors of their day. Booth's family was largely pro-Union, but Booth himself was a fervent supporter of the Confederate cause. After Booth assassinated Lincoln, he led authorities on a 12-day manhunt. He was finally shot and killed by a Union soldier on April 26, 1865, after refusing to surrender at a Virginia farm where he had taken refuge.

Booth's Deringer

Gloria Swift, National Park Service

John Wilkes Booth changed history with this deringer pistol. The .44-caliber bullet that he fired entered Lincoln's brain from behind the left ear and lodged just behind the president's right eye. The bullet not only took the president's life, it also robbed a war-weary nation of an established leader as the country embarked on Reconstruction.

As the doctors bent over to examine Lincoln, one of them called for a knife to cut away Lincoln's vest and shirt in order to search his torso for a wound. William T. Kent, standing nearby, quickly handed over his pocketknife.

Kent returned to the theatre later that night in search of his pocketknife. Allowed in by the guards, Kent made his way to the box where the president had been sitting. When he got down on the floor to search for his knife, he discovered the deringer that Booth had dropped after shooting the president.

Kent immediately turned it over to army investigators who kept it, along with other objects associated with the assassination, at the Judge Advocate General's office until 1940. At that time, the deringer, along with other items relating to Lincoln's assassination, were transferred to the Ford's Theatre Museum for exhibition.

Upon Abraham Lincoln's death, Secretary of War Edwin Stanton pronounced in a shaken voice, "Now he belongs to the ages." Today, Booth's deringer does as well. It evokes the death of our great president and powerfully conjures up the "night of horrors" that started so innocently, and then went unmistakably awry. It speaks to us, sometimes in a whisper, sometimes in a shout, now and for years to come.

— JAY WINIK, Former Council Member, National Endowment for the Humanities
Author, *April 1865: The Month That Saved America*

BOOTH'S BEAUTIES

Booth was carrying these photographs at the time of his capture. The women shown here include two actress friends and his secret fiancée, Lucy Hale (left). Lucy's father, Senator John P. Hale, was a well-known abolitionist.

BOOTH'S DIARY

When Booth fled Ford's Theatre, he carried several items, including an appointment book that he used as a diary. Booth's writings indicate that he expected to be hailed as a hero.

POWELL'S PICKAXE

Powell arrived at the Surratt home with this pickaxe while Mary Surratt was being questioned by police. He claimed he had been hired to dig a ditch. Powell and Surratt were both arrested.

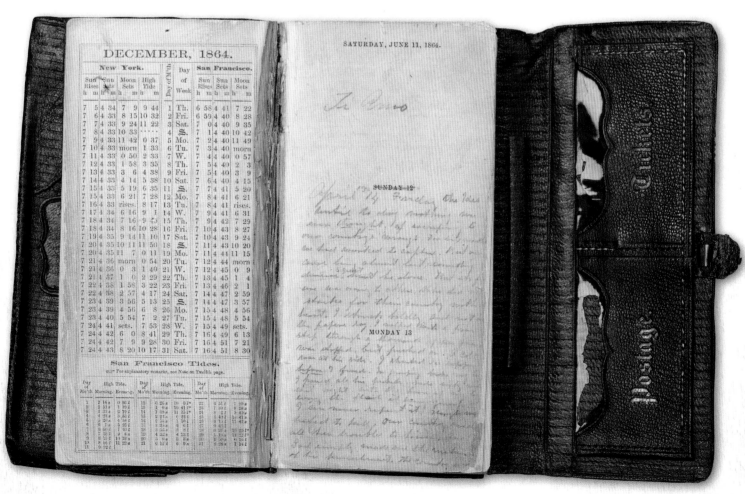

Laura Keene

Stage actress and producer Laura Keene was the first prominent female theatre manager in the United States. Born in London as Mary Moss, Keene came to the United States in 1852 and quickly found success on the American stage. In 1855, she made history by founding her own New York theatre, Laura Keene's Varieties Theatre. Keene brought *Our American Cousin* to Ford's Theatre in 1865, playing Florence Trenchard, the leading role. The show on April 14 was a benefit performance, meaning that Keene would share in the ticket sales. After the assassination, Keene seldom spoke about the events of that fateful night.

Good Friday

ord's Theatre on Tenth Street was a popular venue in Washington. Owner and theatre manager John T. Ford had converted the building from a church into a music hall and playhouse in 1861 and named it "Ford's Athenaeum." When the venue was destroyed by fire the following year, Ford decided to rebuild. Ford's "New Theatre" opened in August 1863.

Because he was a well-known actor who performed at Ford's regularly, John Wilkes Booth had access to Ford's Theatre at any time. He knew every room and secret passage in the building. Since Booth traveled frequently, he often had his mail delivered to Ford's. On Good Friday, April 14, 1865, Booth arrived at the theatre to pick up his mail around 11 a.m. While there, he learned the president and Mrs. Lincoln planned to attend that evening's performance of *Our American Cousin*. Newspapers reported that General Ulysses S. Grant and his wife were expected to accompany the Lincolns.

Booth spent the rest of the day setting his plan in motion. He rented a horse from a nearby stable to prepare for an escape later that night and also attended a dress rehearsal of *Our American Cousin*. At 1 p.m., he visited Mary Surratt at her boardinghouse and gave her a wrapped package containing a set of field glasses and a pair of guns to be delivered to the Surratt family tavern in Surrattsville, Maryland. Booth asked her to tell the tavern keeper that a few gentlemen would come by later that night to pick up the contents of the package. Finally, he met with Powell, Atzerodt and Herold to review their plan.

In the late afternoon, Booth went to the Star Saloon next to Ford's Theatre, where he was seen drinking and laughing with several friends. One of them joked that Booth would never be as great an actor as his father. "When I leave the stage for good," he replied, "I will be the most famous man in America."

BOOTH'S COMPASS
John Wilkes Booth used this compass during his 12-day escape through Maryland and Virginia.

FAMILY OF ACTORS
John Wilkes Booth (left, as Marc Antony) appeared with his brothers, Edwin Booth (center, as Brutus) and Junius Brutus Booth, Jr. (right, as Cassius), in a production of *Julius Caesar* in 1864.

MARY SURRATT
In 1864, Mary Surratt rented out her tavern in Surrattsville, Maryland, and moved to her family's townhouse in Washington, D.C., where she offered rooms for rent.

The Lincoln assassination does not just resonate — it still hurts. There is an almost implacable sense of tragedy about the murder of Abraham Lincoln that even the passage of time doesn't alleviate. The nation does not mourn the way it did in 1865, but it hasn't forgotten. Anywhere in the country a scholar speaking on the Civil War will invariably be asked, "What if Lincoln had lived?" That haunting question has no answer, but it resonates nonetheless.

— MATTHEW PINSKER, Pohanka Chair for Civil War History, Dickinson College
Author, *Lincoln's Sanctuary: Abraham Lincoln and the Soldiers' Home*

THE PRESIDENTIAL BOX
The Lincolns and their party sat in this box at Ford's Theatre, located directly above the stage — putting them as much on public display as the actors themselves.

Playbill and Dress Fragment

James L. Swanson, private collection

When H. Polkinhorn and Son printed the *Our American Cousin* playbill on April 14, 1865, in its shop on D Street near Seventh Street, the sheet of paper was no more than a commonplace piece of theatrical ephemera. It was not even a program for the audience, but rather an advertisement to be handed out in the street that day to drum up ticket sales. Had Lincoln not been shot, the playbill would have been forgotten. But the assassination invested it with unparalleled significance, transforming it into one of the most iconic relics in American history.

Laura Keene's costume, similarly, would have been forgotten or worn for another role. Instead, it became a treasured — if gruesome — keepsake of the famous actress's most infamous performance.

After John Wilkes Booth fled Ford's Theatre, Laura Keene raced from the stage to the Presidential Box, where she discovered that Dr. Charles Leale had laid Abraham Lincoln on the floor. She knelt beside the unconscious, dying president and cradled his head in her lap. Blood from the bullet wound stained her silk costume, adding to the red, yellow, green and blue floral pattern. Soon the dress became an object of morbid curiosity for souvenir hunters.

Unable to destroy the relic, Keene exiled it into the care of her family. The dress vanished long ago, but miraculously, a few treasured remnants survived. According to an accompanying letter of provenance from Keene's grandson, this one was presented to a longtime family friend. The gay floral pattern remains almost as bright as the day the dress was made more than 150 years ago in Chicago by dressmaker Jamie Bullock. But the red bloodstains faded long ago to a pale, rust-brown.

Lincoln's Last Day

riday the 14th was a busy day for the Lincolns. At 8 a.m., the president had breakfast with Mrs. Lincoln, their youngest son, Tad, and their oldest son, Robert, who had just returned from Appomattox, where he served as an aide to General Grant.

After breakfast, Lincoln met with members of his Cabinet and Speaker of the House Schuyler Colfax about Reconstruction policies. He also met with his new minister to Spain, former New Hampshire Senator John P. Hale. During the Cabinet meeting, General Ulysses S. Grant joined the group to discuss Reconstruction. Lincoln said it was "providential" that Congress had adjourned until December as it gave him time to readmit rebellious states while protecting former slaves. Lincoln also recounted a dream in which he was traveling by water toward "an indefinite shore." He took it as a favorable omen, as he had experienced the same dream before several other turning points in the war.

Later in the afternoon, Lincoln took a carriage ride with his wife. Their destination was the Navy Yard in southeast Washington, where they would see the ironclad ship, the U.S.S. *Montauk*. They spent a short time touring the ship and then retraced their route back to the White House. The president was uncharacteristically merry. "Dear husband, you almost startle me by your great cheerfulness," Mary told him.

At the White House, Lincoln ran into Illinois Governor Richard Oglesby and another old friend from Illinois. They came inside to chat, and afterward, Lincoln read aloud to his guests from one of his favorite humorists. The president joined Mary at the dinner table around 7 p.m. and then had a second meeting with Speaker Colfax. As the clock struck 8 p.m., Lincoln confirmed an appointment the next morning with Massachusetts Congressman George Ashmun.

With his business for the day finished, Lincoln walked out of the North Portico to a waiting carriage. Before climbing in, the president turned to his guard, William Henry Crook. Instead of saying his usual farewell, "Good night, Crook," President Lincoln bid the guard an unexpected, "Good-bye, Crook."

A PERSONAL REQUEST
On January 19, 1865, Lincoln wrote to General Grant to ask if his son Robert could serve as his aide in the Union Army.

U.S.S. *MONTAUK*
Abraham and Mary Lincoln toured the U.S.S. *Montauk* on the last day of Lincoln's life. John Wilkes Booth's body would be identified and autopsied on the deck of the *Montauk* nearly two weeks later.

LINCOLN AT HOME
This engraving by William Sartain depicts the Lincoln family. Tad is seated at Lincoln's right and Robert is standing. Willie, who died in 1862, is shown in a portrait.

Mary Lincoln

Mary Lincoln hailed from a prominent family in Kentucky. She met Abraham Lincoln in 1839 and they married in 1842. Her family mirrored the divided nation, with several of her brothers and brothers-in-law fighting for the Confederate Army. In Washington, Mrs. Lincoln found herself unpopular and misunderstood. Some claimed she was a Confederate spy, while others called her renovations to the dilapidated White House "unpatriotic" because of their excess. After losing two sons and her husband, Mrs. Lincoln would suffer one more loss. Her youngest son, Thomas, known as Tad, died of tuberculosis in 1871. For the rest of her life, she struggled with loneliness and depression. She died in 1882 in her sister's home, where she had married Abraham Lincoln 40 years earlier.

Lincoln's Great Coat

Gloria Swift, National Park Service

As Abraham Lincoln readied for his second inaugural in March 1865, he received a gift from Brooks Brothers, a New York men's clothier. The company sent him a beautifully made great coat of fine wool. What made this coat a fitting gift for Lincoln's second inauguration was the design stitched into the silk lining, which reflected Lincoln's hope for his war-torn country. An exquisitely sewn large eagle held a banner in his beak that read, "One Country, One Destiny."

Just six weeks after he wore it to his second inauguration, Lincoln would wear the coat to Ford's Theatre on the night he was assassinated.

The coat was returned to Mary Lincoln after the assassination, but Mrs. Lincoln — unable to bear the sight of the last clothing her husband wore — gave both his suit and the great coat to Alphonse Donn, the Lincolns' favorite usher at the White House. Donn kept the clothes in his possession, allowing only a few special guests to view them. Some snipped a small souvenir from the shoulder of the great coat, where Lincoln's blood had soaked through. It was common practice in the 19th century to retrieve such mementos, but these snips would eventually cause the left sleeve to separate from the coat.

The Donn family kept Lincoln's clothing until 1968, when the American Trucking Association donated $25,000 to the U.S. Capitol Historical Society for the purchase of the suit and great coat. The U.S. Capitol Historical Society then donated the clothes to the National Park Service.

LINCOLN'S LAST RECEPTION
This 1865 lithograph shows the Lincolns greeting guests at a White House reception following Lincoln's second inauguration.

Mary Lincoln's Cloak

Russell Lewis, Chicago History Museum

"Take that woman out and do not let her in again," Secretary of War Edwin M. Stanton curtly demanded when Mary Lincoln collapsed by her dying husband. For the past 150 years, most biographers and historians writing about Lincoln have held to Stanton's order in their narratives. They write about the first assassination of an American president and the nation's loss, not the personal tragedy of a wife losing her husband and the father of her children. But Mary Lincoln's cloak places her front and center in the terrible tragedy that unfolded on April 14, 1865, and reminds us that the couple was devoted to each other.

The black velvet cloak Mrs. Lincoln wore to Ford's Theatre bears five areas of stains, believed to be the blood of Major Henry Rathbone, who bled profusely from a severe knife wound to his arm. After the assassination, Mary Lincoln gave numerous personal items to close friends. It is not surprising that she presented several, including the cloak, to Elizabeth Keckly, her dressmaker, who for six years also served as her personal assistant and confidant.

In 1890 Elizabeth Keckly sold the cloak, which she described as "wet with blood," along with the other gifts from Mary Lincoln, to Chicago candy manufacturer and collector Charles F. Gunther for $250. When Gunther died in 1920, the Chicago Historical Society (now Chicago History Museum) purchased his collection for $150,000, acquiring the cloak and a number of assassination items, including the deathbed, a bloodstained sheet, furniture and artwork from the Petersen House.

For all Americans, this bloodstained cloak bears silent witness to the physical horror of the assassination, when John Wilkes Booth's bullet pierced Lincoln's skull. For Mary Lincoln, the cloak represented both her past and future. Its elegance speaks to her past as a hostess in the White House, and its bloody stains signify her future life in black widow's weeds, seeking help from spiritualists as she mourned the man who had been her "All."

— JEAN BAKER, Professor of History, Goucher College
Author, *Mary Todd Lincoln: A Biography*

THE PRESIDENT'S BOX
Prolific Civil War photographer Mathew Brady took this photograph after the assassination. It was used during modern renovations to re-create the box.

John T. Ford

A Baltimore native and theatrical impresario, John T. Ford rose to prominence in Washington after converting the First Baptist Church on Tenth Street into a successful performance venue in 1861. Ford managed theatre companies in Baltimore and Richmond as well as Washington. He was a leading figure in Baltimore civic life and was close friends with actor John Wilkes Booth. After Lincoln was murdered, Ford and his two brothers, who managed the theatre for him, were thrown into prison for 39 days. They were released when the government determined that they were not involved in the assassination plot. Ford passed away in 1894.

A Night at the Theatre

President Lincoln had few diversions to take his mind off the war, and he relished what relief he could find. One of his favorite activities was attending the theatre. Lincoln frequently patronized Washington theatres, including Ford's. In fact, Lincoln had seen John Wilkes Booth at Ford's Theatre in a production of *The Marble Heart* in 1863.

The Lincolns were looking forward to seeing Laura Keene in her 1,000th performance of *Our American Cousin*. The president and Mrs. Lincoln originally planned to attend with General Ulysses S. Grant and his wife, Julia, but the Grants had decided to leave town that afternoon. The Lincolns invited over a dozen guests before finally receiving an acceptance to their offer from Major Henry Rathbone and his fiancée, Clara Harris.

The Lincolns and their young guests arrived at the theatre at 8:30 p.m., about 15 minutes after the performance of *Our American Cousin* had started. As the party wound its way up the staircase and crossed the Dress Circle to the Presidential Box, the audience cheered and gave the president a standing ovation. Leading actress Laura Keene stopped the performance, and the orchestra played "Hail to the Chief."

Inside the box, Lincoln sat in an upholstered rocking chair with Mary at his right side. During intermission, the president's bodyguard, John Parker, went to the Star Saloon next door for a drink. He did not return for the beginning of Act III. Around 10 p.m., Lincoln reached for Mary's hand.

When Mary wondered aloud what young Clara would think, the president responded, "She won't think anything about it." These were his last words. A few minutes later, John Wilkes Booth entered Ford's Theatre through a backstage door and made his way to the Presidential Box.

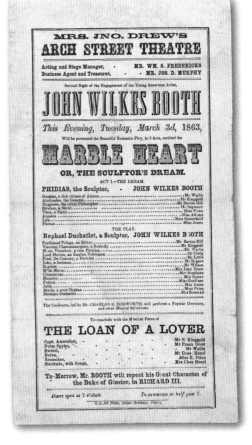

THE MARBLE HEART
John Wilkes Booth headlined *The Marble Heart*, as seen in this March 3, 1863, playbill from Arch Street Theatre in Philadelphia.

ADMIT TWO
These Ford's Theatre tickets were for reserved seating in the Dress Circle on the evening of April 14, 1865.

MUSIC OF THE NIGHT
This violin was played in the orchestra during the ill-fated performance of *Our American Cousin*.

A HERO'S WELCOME
For Lincoln's visit, the Presidential Box was decorated with flags and a portrait of George Washington. The decorations are re-created in the theatre today.

Lincoln's Carriage

Drew Van De Wielle, Studebaker National Museum

Lincoln's transport to Ford's Theatre on April 14 was a barouche, a four-wheeled horse-drawn carriage with a front seat for the driver and passenger seats facing each other. It was built by the Wood Bros. of New York. Sources differ as to when President Lincoln acquired the carriage: The Studebaker Corporation's own files list three different dates. An affidavit from President Lincoln's son Robert Todd Lincoln states that a group of New York citizens gave it to the president shortly after his second inauguration. Another source claims it was presented to President Lincoln in 1861, while the third cites 1863 as the date of acquisition.

Following the assassination, Robert Todd Lincoln sold the carriage to Dr. F. B. Brewer of New York. Clement Studebaker purchased the carriage from Dr. Brewer in 1890 and placed it on display at the Studebaker's Chicago Repository on Michigan Avenue. It traveled to many fairs and expositions, including the 1893 World's Fair in Chicago, where it appeared with Revolutionary War hero Marquis de Lafayette's barouche.

In 1966 the Studebaker Corporation shut down its automotive manufacturing division and donated its 37-vehicle corporate collection, including the Lincoln carriage, to the city of South Bend with the agreement that the city would create a museum. The Lincoln carriage continues to be a highlight of the growing collection at the Studebaker National Museum.

During conservation work in 2008, President Lincoln's monogram was uncovered on both doors. The monogram shows President Lincoln's initials, "AL."

The Assassination

On stage, actor Harry Hawk was just getting to the punch line of the play's best joke when John Wilkes Booth reached the Presidential Box carrying a dagger and a .44-caliber pistol designed by Henry Deringer of Philadelphia. Favored for its small size, the deringer could easily be concealed inside a pocket. Since it fired a round ball instead of a conical-shaped bullet, however, the pistol was only effective at very close range. If fired accurately, the single bullet, weighing nearly 1 ounce, could be deadly.

Booth approached the president's footman, Charles Forbes, who allowed him to enter the box. As a famous actor, almost any door in Washington was open to Booth. Once inside the box, he wedged the door shut with the leg of a wooden music stand that he had placed behind the door earlier in the day. Booth then took aim, standing a few feet behind the president, who was leaning forward, enjoying the play. When Hawk delivered the big punch line, "You sockdologizing old mantrap!" the audience exploded into uproarious laughter and Booth pulled the trigger.

After the gun fired, Booth dropped the pistol on the floor of the theatre box. He took out his dagger and moved swiftly to jump over the balustrade, grappling momentarily with Lincoln's guest, Major Henry Rathbone. Booth cut Rathbone's arm in the brief scuffle, gravely injuring the young man.

Booth leapt out of the theatre box and caught the spur of his boot on the Treasury Guard flag displayed on the center column of the box. He crashed down onto the stage. As he leapt up, some theatregoers heard him shout the Virginia state motto, "Sic semper tyrannis!" (Thus always to tyrants!) Others heard, "The South is avenged!" As Booth tore across the stage, he ran into orchestra master William Withers, Jr., who was standing in the wings. Booth slashed at him with his dagger, slicing two holes in Withers's jacket and knocking him to the floor. Booth then escaped out a rear exit door into an alley.

BOOTH'S DAGGER
Booth used this dagger to slash Major Henry Rathbone's arm. It is engraved with the words *liberty* and *America*.

RATHBONE'S BLOODY GLOVES
The Lincolns' guest Henry Rathbone wore these gloves to the theatre. The bloodstains came from the wounds Rathbone sustained during his scuffle with Booth.

LEAP FROM THE BOX
Booth, pictured jumping from the box, later wrote in his journal, "I struck boldly, and … shouted Sic semper before I fired. In jumping [I] broke my leg."

A HEROIC EFFORT
After the shot rang out, Rathbone sprang from his seat and tried to wrestle Booth to the ground. Booth escaped his grasp by slashing Rathbone's arm to the bone.

Henry Rathbone

Major Henry Rathbone studied law and later joined the Union Army. He served in the battles of Antietam and Fredericksburg. He and his fiancée, Clara Harris, were sitting in the Presidential Box at Ford's Theatre when John Wilkes Booth assassinated President Lincoln. Rathbone yelled, "Stop that man!" and jumped out of his seat to chase Booth. He was badly injured when Booth attacked him with a knife. Rathbone also sustained emotional scars and never forgave himself for letting Booth escape. Eventually, Rathbone became violently delusional. On December 23, 1883, Rathbone shot and stabbed his wife to death then stabbed himself. When the police arrived, he claimed there were people living behind the pictures on the wall. He died in an asylum 28 years later.

Clara Harris

Clara Harris was a friend of Mary Lincoln and moved in Washington's highest social circles. Her father, Ira Harris, was a senator from New York. Her mother died when Clara was young, and her father remarried a widow, Pauline Rathbone, who already had two sons, Henry and Jared. Though they were stepsiblings who had grown up together, Henry Rathbone and Clara Harris fell in love. Their engagement began not long before they attended the theatre with the Lincolns. They went on to marry and have three children. In 1883, while living in Germany, Clara died tragically at the hand of her husband, who had succumbed to madness after years of regret that he had been unable to prevent Lincoln's assassination.

The Bunting Flag

Lori Strelecki, Pike County Historical Society

In preparation for Lincoln's visit to Ford's Theatre on April 14, a large flag — measuring more than 8 feet high and 12 feet long — was hung as decorative bunting on the front of the Presidential Box. After John Wilkes Booth shot President Lincoln, the flag was pulled from the balustrade and used to cushion the president's head as he lay unconscious in the box. The flag became stained with his blood.

Five flags in total were displayed in Ford's that fateful night. All five of them were removed by souvenir hunters. The bloodstained flag was taken by Thomas Gourlay, an actor in the show that night and a part-time manager for Ford's Theatre. When Thomas died, he left the flag to his daughter Jennie Gourlay, who had also been on stage that night. Her name, along with Laura Keene's, appears on the *Our American Cousin* playbill.

Jennie married and moved to Milford, Pennsylvania, in 1888. She preserved the blood-stained flag, along with several costumes, one of which she planned to wear on the night of the assassination. The small town's residents were aware that Jennie had this somewhat macabre artifact, but she very rarely spoke of the assassination.

Jennie died in 1928 and left the flag to her son, Vivian Paul Struthers. Struthers gave the flag and Jennie Gourlay's stage costumes to the Pike County Historical Society in 1954. They have been in the society's possession ever since.

AN ASSASSIN'S ESCAPE
Booth escaped through the backstage door of Ford's Theatre, where he had left a horse waiting.

Laura Keene's Cuff

Harry Rubenstein, National Museum of American History

As John Wilkes Booth escaped from Ford's Theatre, the audience erupted into chaos. The play's leading actress, Laura Keene, approached the front of the stage and pleaded with the crowd to remain calm. Cast member Helen Truman recounted, "The shouts, groans, curses, smashing of seats, screams of women, shuffling of feet and cries of terror created a pandemonium that … through all the ages will stand out in my memory as the hell of hells." In the confusion, someone called to bring the president water. Keene ran to her dressing room, grabbed a pitcher of water and made her way to the Presidential Box. As she cradled the president's head in her lap, drops of Lincoln's blood stained her cuff and dress.

Rather than return to her home in Georgetown, Keene stayed at the nearby Metropolitan Hotel. That night she cut the stained cuff from the sleeve of her dress. The next day, as news of the president's death gripped the city, Keene met with her husband's nephew, M. J. Adler, and presented him with the cuff. It was made of fine linen with pearl buttons and stained with Lincoln's blood. The family saved this memento of Keene's role in that tragic night as a cherished possession. The cuff was passed down to Adler's daughter, Mary Adler Thompson, who bequeathed it to the Smithsonian Institution following her death in 1962.

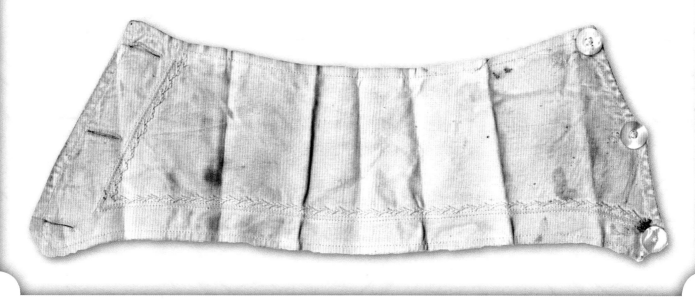

If the Civil War was, as Lincoln believed, our greatest national challenge, the resolution of the war would require a hand on the presidential wheel that was as perceptive and balanced as Lincoln's. The removal of that hand allowed the ensuing years of Reconstruction to drift from one destructive shoal to another, creating a racial canker that poisons the nation's spirit today. Lincoln's murder haunts us, both for how easily it might have been prevented, and for the uncertainty all Americans were left to live with in its wake.

— ALLEN C. GUELZO, Henry R. Luce Professor of the Civil War Era, Gettysburg College
Author, *Fateful Lightning: A New History of the Civil War and Reconstruction*

LAURA KEENE
Laura Keene's productions often had record-setting runs. She debuted *Our American Cousin* in 1858 and played the role of Florence Trenchard more than 1,000 times.

Charles Leale

Charles Augustus Leale served as an assistant surgeon for the Union Army. On April 11, 1865, Leale heard Lincoln deliver what was to be his last speech from the balcony of the White House. Fascinated by the president's countenance, Leale decided to study the man he called the "Savior of His Country" at the next opportunity. When Leale learned that Lincoln would attend *Our American Cousin* at Ford's Theatre, he purchased a ticket in the Dress Circle, where he sat close enough to the Presidential Box to see Lincoln. Leale was the first physician to tend to Lincoln after the assassination and was part of the honor guard in the president's grand funeral procession. Leale practiced medicine until his death in 1932.

A Mortal Wound

*T*he bullet fired by John Wilkes Booth lodged behind President Lincoln's right eye. As theatregoers began to realize that the gunshot and screaming were not part of the performance, pandemonium broke out. The audience ran for the exits as Mary Lincoln's cries for help pierced the air. Laura Keene begged the crowd to stay calm, pleading, "For God's sake … keep your places and all will be well!"

Mrs. Lincoln held her husband in the rocker, sobbing, as Rathbone, already weak from blood loss, finally managed to remove the music stand leg that Booth had used to bar the door. Once the door opened, Dr. Charles Leale burst into the Presidential Box. Leale, a 23-year-old doctor just six weeks out of medical school, saw immediately that the situation was bleak. Lincoln's eyes were closed, and he was unresponsive. Leale examined the back of the president's head and discovered a large clot of blood.

As Leale performed his initial assessment, a second doctor and family friend of the Lincolns, Charles Taft, was lifted from the stage into the box. With the chaos in the theatre, this was the quickest way to reach the president's side.

The two doctors moved Lincoln to the floor and felt for a pulse, but there was none. Leale began to resuscitate the president while Taft lifted his arms. With their efforts, Lincoln's heart began beating again, but Leale's diagnosis was grim: "His wound is mortal; it is impossible for him to recover."

Having determined that the White House was too far to take the president, Leale and Taft ordered soldiers to carry Lincoln to the street, where they found their way to William Petersen's boardinghouse. The soldiers carried the president inside to a small back room and laid the president's tall frame diagonally across a four-poster bed. Leale, Taft and nearly a dozen other doctors tried to make Lincoln comfortable. Mrs. Lincoln and her eldest son, Robert Todd Lincoln, spent a sleepless night in the front parlor, checking frequently on the president. At 7:22 a.m. on April 15, President Lincoln was pronounced dead. Secretary of War Edwin Stanton is said to have uttered, "Now he belongs to the ages."

STAINED PILLOW
At the Petersen House, Lincoln's head was laid on several pillows. This one shows the bloodstains from his gunshot wound.

LINCOLN'S LAST HOUR
This lithograph, circa 1865, shows Lincoln on his deathbed in the Petersen House accompanied by doctors, his son Robert and various members of his Cabinet.

CONFEDERATE BILL

This $5 bill was the only money in Lincoln's wallet that night. Historians speculate that the Confederate bill may have been a souvenir of his visit to the fallen Confederate capital, Richmond, just days before.

LINCOLN'S WALLET

Lincoln carried several items in his pockets on the night he was shot, including this wallet. The wallet contained a $5 Confederate note (pictured) and eight newspaper clippings that spoke favorably of the Lincoln administration.

PETERSEN HOUSE

Lincoln died in this back bedroom at the Petersen House. More than 90 people came through the house to pay their last respects to the president that night.

Lincoln's Deathbed

Russell Lewis, Chicago History Museum

The simple walnut spool bed dominated the cramped room at the back of the first-floor hall in the Petersen board-inghouse. It was common furniture, typical for a boarder's room. Lincoln's 6-foot 4-inch frame, however, was too large for the bed, and he was placed diagonally across it. The bed cradled the mortally wounded president for the next eight-and-a-half hours, but the awkward and undignified positioning of Lincoln with his feet protruding from under the coverlet heightened the despair that had descended upon the room. At just after 7:22 a.m. on the morn-ing of April 15, Abraham Lincoln died.

The notoriety of the house after Lincoln's death proved to be a disaster for the Petersen family. People flocked to see the bed and frequently cut or tore off souvenirs. Borders moved out, and in 1871 William Petersen committed sui-cide and his wife, Ana, died of a prolonged illness. The Petersen children sold the house and auctioned its contents.

William Boyd bought the bed and other furniture for his brother, Andrew, a publisher and an accomplished Lincoln collector. In 1889, Andrew Boyd sold the bed and the furniture to Charles Gunther, who was establishing a Civil War museum in Chicago. By selling the items to Gunther, Boyd was placing them "in safe hands where they would be secure for all future time and where the public could see them." The Chicago Historical Society (now the Chicago History Museum) pur-chased Gunther's collec-tion in 1920, and true to Boyd's wishes, the bed has been on view in the museum ever since.

In my case and the case of thousands and thousands of others, Abraham Lincoln is preeminent because he signed the Emancipation Proclamation, setting my grandfather and all of his lineage free. Once free, my grandfather walked 100 miles across Kentucky to Berea College and the college let him in. He graduated, laying the groundwork for gaining middle-class status for my family. It is ahistorical to ask "What if?" but you have to think that Reconstruction would have unfolded differently had Abraham Lincoln lived.

— JULIAN BOND, Social Activist and Civil Rights Leader
Former Board Chairman, National Association for the Advancement of Colored People

Dr. Leale's Letter

John Sellers, Shapell Manuscript Foundation

Dr. Charles A. Leale, the author of this eight-page letter, was one of three physicians to offer his services to the mortally wounded President Lincoln. As the first on the scene, professional etiquette placed him in control of the president's care. He remained in charge until the Lincolns' family doctor, Robert K. Stone, arrived later that evening.

It is obvious from the content of Leale's letter to Dr. Dwight Dudley, a former colleague and lifelong friend, that Dudley was seeking firsthand information on the Lincoln assassination. Leale devoted most of his response to the subject, but he also offered some interesting insight into the mental condition of the conspirators, whose trial he attended. He wrote of the assassination:

> *"[I] told Mrs. L. that I was a surgeon. When she asked me to do what I could he was then in a profound Coma, pulse could not be felt, eyes closed, stertorous breathing. … As soon as his shoulder was laid bare and no wound discovered I examined his head and first felt a protuberance. … I then knew it was fatal and told the bystanders that it was a mortal wound."*

Leale may have included more medical detail in his account to Dudley because he and Dudley had first became acquainted while serving as medical cadets at the U.S. Army General Hospital in Elmira, New York. There, both men earned the title of Acting Assistant Surgeon, which entitled them to the rank of lieutenant in the Volunteer Army. Dudley later went to the medical school at Columbia University, and Leale to the Bellevue Hospital Medical College.

IN HIS WORDS

Leale explained, "[I] saw Booth enter the box and heard the report of the pistol then saw him jump from the box. … I immediately ran to the box and there saw the President sitting in the armchair with his head thrown back."

I was appointed Executive Officer and am at present in charge. I had charge of the President until his family physician arrived. That night was the only time that I have been to the Theatre since I came here and then partly to see Mr. Lincoln and Gen Grant. I took a seat in the Dress Circle near the President's Box saw Booth enter the box heard the report of the pistol then saw him jump from the box with his draw dagger and rush across the stage. I immediately ran to the box and there saw the President sitting in the arm chair with his head thrown back on one side was Mrs. L. and on the other Miss Harris

The former was holding his head and crying bitterly for a Surgeon while the others there were standing crying for stimulants water etc not one going for anything. While going towards him I sent one for Brandy and another for Water, then told Mrs. L. that I was a Surgeon, when she asked me to do what I could. He was then in a profound coma, pulse could not be felt, eyes closed, stertorous breathing. I immediately with assistance placed him in a recumbent position on the floor. While doing this I put my hand on a part of his coat near the left shoulder saturated with blood supposing him to have been stabbed. I asked

Just as the joy that greeted the return of peace yielded to sorrow inspired by the murder of the president, the grief of April 1865 inspired a new birth of freedom and the emergence of the re-United States as the world's strongest democracy. Haunted as we are by what might have been, we were ultimately made stronger, not weaker, by Lincoln's life and perhaps even his death.

— HAROLD HOLZER, Chairman, Lincoln Bicentennial Foundation
Author, *Lincoln and the Power of the Press: The War for Public Opinion*

Flight and Inquisition

The hunt for Booth and his collaborators started immediately, led by Secretary of War Edwin Stanton from the parlor of the Petersen House. Over the course of the investigation, dozens of individuals, including John T. Ford, the proprietor of Ford's Theatre, would be arrested and imprisoned. Eventually, eight people would be tried and convicted of conspiracy.

As Booth fled Ford's Theatre the night of April 14, his co-conspirators attempted to put their own pieces of the deadly plan into action, but with less success. George Atzerodt spent the evening drinking at the bar in the Kirkwood Hotel, trying to work up the courage to assassinate Vice President Andrew Johnson. He eventually left the hotel and wandered the streets, throwing his knife into the gutter.

Lewis Powell (also known as Lewis Paine or Payne) was assigned to kill Secretary of State William Seward. Powell arrived at Seward's home with David Herold, claiming he was there to deliver a prescription to Seward who was in bed recovering from a carriage accident. When Seward's son, Frederick, stopped him on the stairs, Powell clubbed him across the head with his revolver. Powell then burst into the Secretary's room, stabbing Seward in the face and neck. The jaw splint that Seward was wearing because of the accident saved his life.

Meanwhile, Booth was on the run. He met up with Herold on the road out of Washington and traveled to Mary Surratt's tavern in Maryland, picking up the field glasses (binoculars) and Spencer carbine rifle he had asked her to deliver earlier that day. On April 15, Booth and Herold stopped to see Dr. Samuel Mudd, who treated the ankle Booth had shattered while making his escape. For 12 days, Booth and Herold fled through Maryland and into Virginia.

The men were apprehended on April 26, 1865, in a tobacco barn near Port Royal, just south of the Rappahannock River. Herold gave himself up, but Booth refused to surrender. He was shot and killed after the barn he was hiding in was set ablaze. In his final breaths, Booth uttered, "Useless, useless!" as he gazed at his hands.

MILITARY TRIBUNAL
Secretary of War Edwin Stanton favored a quick military trial, overseen by a commission of generals, colonels and majors. Of the eight conspirators tried, four were sentenced to death.

BOOTH'S RIFLE
Booth carried this Spencer carbine rifle during his escape. The canvas sling allowed him to wear it over his shoulder.

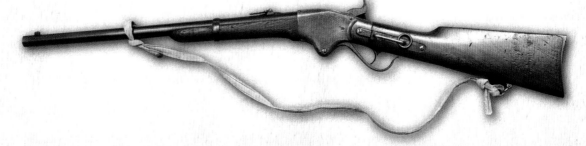

The Conspirators

John Wilkes Booth died in Virginia at the end of the manhunt, but his co-conspirators were apprehended and subjected to a military tribunal. When Booth and Herold were found hiding in a tobacco barn near Port Royal, Herold surrendered himself to soldiers from the 16th New York Cavalry. After brutally stabbing Secretary of State William Seward, Lewis Powell fled the crime scene and hid near the Navy Yard Bridge for three days. On April 17, he arrived at Mary Surratt's boardinghouse, where police were questioning her. Immediately suspicious of Powell's involvement in the conspiracy, the authorities arrested him. George Atzerodt did not follow through with his part of the plan to kill Vice President Andrew Johnson, but the police received a tip from a hotel employee and found weapons in his abandoned hotel room. Atzerodt was arrested on April 20 at his cousin's home in Germantown, Maryland. The military tribunal, which lasted from May to June, returned death sentences for David Herold, Lewis Powell, George Atzerodt and Mary Surratt. They were hanged on July 7, 1865, at the Old Arsenal Penitentiary (part of today's Fort McNair) in Washington. Dr. Samuel Mudd escaped hanging by one vote. He was sent to Fort Jefferson, 70 miles west of Key West, Florida, along with three other conspirators: Edman Spangler, Michael O'Laughlen and Samuel Arnold.

BOOTH'S BOOT
On April 15, Booth arrived at Dr. Samuel Mudd's house in need of care for his injured leg. Mudd cut the boot from Booth's swollen ankle. Five days later, investigators found the boot at Mudd's house.

DR. SAMUEL MUDD
Mudd, who also introduced Booth to conspirator John Surratt, escaped hanging by one vote.

DR. MUDD'S HOUSE
After picking up weapons in Surrattsville, Maryland, John Wilkes Booth and David Herold reached the farm of Dr. Samuel Mudd in Waldorf, Maryland.

Contents of Lincoln's Pockets

Mark Dimunation, Library of Congress

At 7:22 a.m. on April 15, 1865, Abraham Lincoln, 16th president of the United States, took his last breath. Edwin Stanton, Secretary of War, is reported to have said, "Now he belongs to the ages." A lock of the president's hair was cut at Mary Lincoln's request. Robert Todd Lincoln was given the contents of his father's pockets.

It was, for the most part, a collection of ordinary items: two pairs of eyeglasses; a chamois lens polisher; an ivory and silver pocketknife; a large white Irish linen handkerchief (slightly used) with "A. Lincoln" embroidered in red; a gold quartz watch fob without a watch; a new silk-lined leather wallet containing a pencil; a Confederate $5 bill; and several newspaper clippings detailing unrest in the Confederate Army, emancipation in Missouri, the Union Party platform of 1864 and an article on the presidency by John Bright.

Through association with tragedy, these objects became relics and were kept in the Lincoln family for more than 70 years. They joined the Library of Congress collection in 1937 as part of a gift from Lincoln's granddaughter, Mary Lincoln Isham. The objects were not put on display until February 12, 1976, when then-Librarian of Congress Daniel Boorstin thought their exposure would humanize a man who had become "mythologically engulfed." Since their first public display, the contents of Lincoln's pockets have become one of the collections visitors to the Library of Congress most often ask to see.

Lincoln delivered his second inaugural address one month before he died, asking the nation to move forward with "malice toward none" and "charity for all." Many interpreted these words to pertain to the vanquished Confederates, but African Americans likely understood them to mean that the nation should honor black freedom and equality. With Lincoln's characteristic subtlety and diplomacy, the second inaugural address called not merely for peace, but for justice. Lincoln's assassination was a monumental loss in the fractured progress of American freedom and equality.

— MARTHA HODES, Professor of History, New York University
Author, *Mourning Lincoln*

EMANCIPATION PROCLAMATION
This 1864 print of the Emancipation Proclamation — one of Lincoln's greatest legacies — depicts the evils of slavery at left and life after emancipation at right.

Legacy

braham Lincoln left a lasting legacy on the people of the United States and throughout the world: dedication to the republic, commitment to equality and belief in the strength of the Declaration of Independence and the Constitution. Through steadfast devotion to his principles, tireless leadership and eloquently worded rhetoric, President Lincoln saved the Union and ended legal slavery in the United States.

Lincoln's death rocked the nation, which had already been torn apart by four years of war. Two days after his assassination, on Easter Sunday, parishioners flocked to churches in black mourning attire. Preachers called the president a martyr, comparing him to another whose murder took place on Good Friday. Northerners were shocked and angry, whereas Southern reaction was mixed. Millions of Americans paid tribute as Lincoln's funeral train passed through the country to his final resting place in Springfield, Illinois.

LINCOLN MEMORIAL
Dedicated in 1922, the Lincoln Memorial has become a rallying place for citizens striving toward a united, free and equal society.

Kings and prime ministers from around the world sent condolences to the United States. An official proclamation from the Republic of Liberia, where many former slaves from the United States had resettled, mourned Lincoln as "not only the ruler of his own people, but a father to millions of a race stricken and oppressed." A group of Prussian laborers noted that the U.S. flag would forever symbolize "the cause of freedom and celebration."

In the wake of the assassination, the Union remained fragile. Vice President Andrew Johnson assumed the presidency and faced the challenge of reconstructing the nation. Fierce debates erupted in Congress and across the country over how severely to punish the states that had seceded and how to incorporate former slaves as American citizens.

The Reconstruction Acts of 1867 set forth the process of readmitting the former Confederate states, but the legislation was controversial. Two new constitutional amendments extended rights specifically to African Americans for the first time. The 14th Amendment granted them citizenship, and the 15th Amendment prevented states from denying African-American men the right to vote. True equal rights for African Americans would not make significant progress until the Civil Rights era of the mid-20th century, and remain part of our nation's struggle today.

JOHNSON'S INAUGURATION
After Lincoln's death, Andrew Johnson took the presidential oath of office in the parlor of his hotel, the Kirkwood House, on April 15, 1865.

Lincoln's Cufflink

James Cornelius, Abraham Lincoln Presidential Library and Museum

Dr. Charles Sabin Taft was, by chance, the second medical man to reach the Presidential Box. John Wilkes Booth had barred the door of the box, so Taft had to be lifted into the box from the stage level.

When he appeared over the edge of the box, Mary Lincoln beheld a welcome friend amidst strangers. The Tafts were family friends of the Lincolns; they had spent Christmas 1861 together, and Dr. Taft's younger brothers, Bud and Holly, often played with Willie and Tad Lincoln in the White House, minded by his sister Julia. Willie's death on February 20, 1862, had ended the children's play but not the families' friendship.

Taft wrote in *Century* magazine's February 1893 issue that the "gold-and-onyx initial sleeve-button" he removed while stripping the president's shirt in search of wounds "was subsequently presented to [him] by Mrs. Lincoln."

Taft gave it to his son, who later sold it to leading Lincoln collector Major William Lambert. Lambert gave the treasure a new home: a custom-made silver box with a beveled glass cover and black velvet bed. The box's top edge is inscribed "Abraham Lincoln / April 14th 1865." On the underside an inscription in minute cursive reads:

> *"Enclosed sleeve button worn by President Lincoln April 14th 1865 was given by Mrs. Lincoln to Dr. Taft, an attending surgeon who had removed it in search for wound. Bought from his son C. C. Taft by W. H. Lambert March 11th 1908."*

After 1914 the button passed through three owners' hands before becoming part of the Abraham Lincoln Presidential Library and Museum collection in 2007.

EXTRA! EXTRA!
The news of Lincoln's murder sent shock waves through the nation, as seen in this clipping.

COURIER---EXTRA.

National Calamity!

Lincoln & Seward Assassinated ! !

WASHINGTON, April 15, 1865.

President Lincoln was shot through the head last night, and died this morning.— The Assassin is supposed to be Wilkes Booth the Actor. About the same time a desperado called at Secretary Seward's, pretending to be a messenger from his physician Being refused admittance, he attacked Frederick Seward, son of the Secretary, knocking down the male attendant, and cut Mr. Seward's throat, the wound was not at first considered fatal. Letters found in Booth's trunk shows that this assassination was contemplated before the fourth of March but fell through from some cause or other. The wildest excitement prevails at Washington. Vice President's and residence of the different Secretaries are closely guarded.

LATER—Seward died this A. M. 9:45.   E. M. STANTON, Sec'y of War.

This sad intelligence falls like a dark pall on the hearts of the people so joyous and hopeful, yesterday, so terribly overwhelmed to-day. What rebels in Richmond dare not do, their accomplices and sympathizers have accomplished in our own capitol.

NOTICE.

All who abhor assassination, deplore murder, and detest the "deep damnation" of the taking off of our Chief Magistrate and Secretary of State, and who sincerely grieve for the great and good men gone are called on to meet

ON THE PUBLIC SQUARE,

AT

3 O'clock, this afternoon, April 15, 1865.

MAYHEM AND MISPRINTS
In the mayhem following the assassination, the facts about the events of April 14th and 15th were often misprinted. For instance, this broadside erroneously states that William Seward was also killed.

LINCOLN'S FUNERAL TRAIN
Lincoln's funeral train traveled through 180 cities and towns in seven states before arriving at his hometown of Springfield, Illinois.

THE PRESIDENT'S FUNERAL
Thirteen cities held elaborate funerals for President Lincoln. This image captured the procession in New York City on April 25, 1865.

Where Lincoln's Legacy Lives

*F*ord's Theatre celebrates the life and legacy of Abraham Lincoln, the nation's 16th president. Restored to its 1865 appearance, Ford's is a working theatre, historical monument, museum and education center that aims to teach the public about Lincoln's legacy.

The historic site faced multiple challenges following Lincoln's death. The public clamored for the theatre to close, and the U.S. government seized the property, paying John Ford $100,000 in compensation. The building was subsequently used for office and storage space by the War Department. On June 9, 1893, the third floor of the building collapsed, killing 22 government workers. After the damage was repaired, the building was used as a warehouse.

Ford's Theatre might have remained a nondescript building if not for the efforts of a few individuals: Osborn Oldroyd, who collected the artifacts that make up the majority of the museum's collections; Democratic National Committeeman Melvin Hildreth, Jr., and Republican Senator Milton Young, who lobbied for decades to save the theatre; and Frankie Hewitt, who formed the Ford's Theatre Society and served as the founding executive producer. During Hewitt's 35-year tenure, Ford's Theatre began producing shows that emphasized the diversity of the American experience.

In 1964, Congress approved funds for the restoration of the site. Four years later, Ford's Theatre reopened as a National Park Service historic property, museum and working theatre. Ford's underwent a major renovation in 2008, adding new museum exhibits that focused on Lincoln's inaugural arrival in Washington, Lincoln's role as an orator and an emancipator, Civil War milestones and generals, the city of Washington during the Civil War and the years of Lincoln's presidency. In 2012, Ford's Theatre Society opened the Center for Education and Leadership, located across the street from the theatre and adjacent to the historic Petersen House. The center explores Lincoln's values and principles, examining his legacy through both exhibits and two floors of education studios, which feature post-visit workshops, after-school programs and teacher professional development. Together, these elements create a living memorial to the nation's most beloved president.

MEMORIALIZING LINCOLN
The third floor of the Center for Education and Leadership explores the memorialization and evolving legacy of Abraham Lincoln.

A TOWERING LEGACY
The tower of books in the Center for Education and Leadership represents just a fraction of the thousands of books written about Abraham Lincoln.

Ford's Theatre celebrates the legacy of President Abraham Lincoln and explores the American experience through theatre and education. A working theatre, historical monument, world-class museum and learning center, Ford's Theatre is the premier destination in Washington, D.C., to explore and celebrate Lincoln's ideals and leadership principles: courage, integrity, tolerance, equality and creative expression. Ford's Theatre is operated through a public/private partnership with the National Park Service and the private non-profit 501(c)(3) Ford's Theatre Society.

Paul Tetreault, Director
Kristin Fox-Siegmund, Director of Programming
Heather Hoagland, Museum Assistant
Tracey Avant, Curator of Exhibitions
Gary Erskine, Art Director
Cait Reizman, Exhibitions Intern
Elena Popchock, Exhibitions Intern

511 Tenth Street, NW
Washington, DC 20004
www.fords.org | 202-347-4833

ISBN: 978-1-935442-48-6
Printed in the United States of America
10 9 8 7 6 5 4 3 2 1

The Lincoln Assassination at Ford's Theatre: Now He Belongs to the Ages was developed by Beckon Books in cooperation with Ford's Theatre. Beckon develops and publishes custom books for leading cultural attractions, corporations and nonprofit organizations. Beckon Books is an imprint of Southwestern Publishing Group, Inc., 2451 Atrium Way, Nashville, TN 37214. Southwestern Publishing Group, Inc., is a wholly owned subsidiary of Southwestern, Inc., Nashville, TN.

Christopher G. Capen, President, Beckon Books
Betsy Holt, Development Director
Vicky Shea, Art Director
Kristin Connelly, Managing Editor
Jennifer Benson, Proofreader
www.beckonbooks.com | 877-311-0155

PHOTO CREDITS

Photos identified top to bottom, left to right.
p. 2: Photo © Maxwell McKenzie; p. 3: Photo © Maxwell McKenzie; p. 4: Library of Congress, Prints and Photographs Division, LC-DIG-ppmsca-19301; p. 6a: Library of Congress, Prints and Photographs Division, LC-DIG-ppmsca-23718; p. 6b: Library of Congress, Prints and Photographs Division, LC-DIG-ppmsca-19190; p. 7a: The Granger Collection, NYC, Image No. 0063516; p. 7b: Library of Congress, Prints and Photographs Division, LC-USZ62-25166; p. 7c: Penn State University Libraries; p. 8a: Library of Congress, Prints and Photographs Division, LC-DIG-ds-05202; p. 8b: Library of Congress, Prints and Photographs Division, LC-USZ62-86311; p. 9: Division of Political History, National Museum of American History, Smithsonian Institution; p. 10a: Carol M. Highsmith's America, Library of Congress, Prints and Photographs Division, LC-DIG-highsm-04740; p. 10b: Library of Congress, Prints and Photographs Division, LC-DIG-ppmsca-35254; p. 10c: Library of Congress, Prints and Photographs Division, LC-DIG-cwpb-04218; p. 10d: Library of Congress, Prints and Photographs Division, LC-DIG-cwpb-04210; p. 11a: Library of Congress, Prints and Photographs Division, LC-DIG-cwpbh-03432; p. 11b: Library of Congress, Prints and Photographs Division, LC-DIG-ppmsca-23892; p. 12: Carol M. Highsmith's America, Library of Congress, Prints and Photographs Division, LC-DIG-highsm-04710; p. 13a: Carol M. Highsmith's America, Library of Congress, Prints and Photographs Division, LC-DIG-highsm-04748; p. 13b: Carol M. Highsmith's America, Library of Congress, Prints and Photographs Division, LC-DIG-highsm-04763; p. 13c: Carol M. Highsmith's America, Library of Congress, Prints and Photographs Division, LC-DIG-highsm-04718; p. 14a: Library of Congress, Prints and Photographs Division, LC-USZ62-47370; p. 14b: Ford's Theatre Society, FTS 011.1.12p; 15a: Carol M. Highsmith's America, Library of Congress, Prints and Photographs Division, LC-DIG-highsm-04714; p. 15b: Brown University Library; p. 15c: Surratt House Museum, MNCPPC; p. 16: Carol M. Highsmith's America, Library of Congress, Prints and Photographs Division, LC-DIG-highsm-11820; p. 17a: Photograph by Gary Erskine, courtesy of James Swanson; p. 17b: Photograph by Gary Erskine, courtesy of James Swanson; p. 18a: Shapell Manuscript Foundation, www.shapell.org; p. 18b: New Jersey State Archives; p. 19a: Library of Congress, Prints and Photographs Division, LC-DIG-pga-03267; p. 19b: Library of Congress, Prints and Photographs Division, LC-DIG-cwpbh-03451; p. 20a: Photo by Carol Highsmith for the National Park Service; p. 20b: Library of Congress, Prints and Photographs Division, LC-DIG-pga-01590; p. 21: Chicago History Museum, ICHi-52434; p. 22a: Library of Congress, Prints and Photographs Division, LC-DIG-cwpb-02961; p. 22b: National Park Service; p. 23a: Mrs. Jno. Drew's Arch Street Theatre Broadside, Playbill Collection [3131], Historical Society of Pennsylvania; p. 23b: Carol M. Highsmith's America, Library of Congress, Prints and Photographs Division, LC-DIG-highsm-04713; p. 23c: Carol M. Highsmith's America, Library of Congress, Prints and Photographs Division, LC-DIG-highsm-04702; p. 24: Carol M. Highsmith's America, Library of Congress, Prints and Photographs Division, LC-DIG-highsm-04783; p. 25: Studebaker National Museum, South Bend, IN; p. 26a: Carol M. Highsmith's America, Library of Congress, Prints and Photographs Division, LC-DIG-highsm-04709; p. 26b: Carol M. Highsmith's America, Library of Congress, Prints and Photographs Division, LC-DIG-highsm-04735; p. 26c: Library of Congress, Rare Book and Special Collections Division, Alfred Whital Stern Collection of Lincolniana; p. 27a: Library of Congress, Prints and Photographs Division, LC-USZC4-1155; p. 27b: Lincoln Financial Foundation Collection, courtesy of the Allen County Public Library and Indiana State Museum; p. 28a: © CORBIS; p. 28b: National Archives photo no. 111-B-4246 (Brady Collection); p. 29a: Photograph by Tamara Singer, courtesy of the Pike County Historical Society; p. 29b: Illinois History and Lincoln Collections, University of Illinois Library; p. 30: Division of Political History, National Museum of American History, Smithsonian Institution; p. 31: Library of Congress, Prints and Photographs Division, LC-DIG-cwpbh-01959; p. 32a: Photographs in the Carol M. Highsmith Archive, Library of Congress, Prints and Photographs Division, LC-DIG-highsm-12344; p. 32b: Library of Congress, Prints and Photographs Division, LC-DIG-cwpbh-03276; p. 33a: Carol M. Highsmith's America, Library of Congress, Prints and Photographs Division, LC-DIG-highsm-15042; p. 33b: Library of Congress, Rare Book and Special Collections Division, Alfred Whital Stern Collection of Lincolniana; p. 34a: Library of Congress, Rare Book and Special Collections Division; p. 34b: Library of Congress, Rare Book and Special Collections Division; p. 34c: Photo © Maxwell McKenzie; p. 35: Chicago History Museum, ICHi-68466; p. 36: Shapell Manuscript Foundation, www.shapell.org; p. 37: Shapell Manuscript Foundation, www.shapell.org; p. 38a: Library of Congress, Prints and Photographs Division, LC-DIG-ppmsca-35257; p. 38b: Carol M. Highsmith's America, Library of Congress, Prints and Photographs Division, LC-DIG-highsm-04762; p. 39: Library of Congress, Prints and Photographs Division, LC-DIG-cwpb-04229; p. 40a: Carol M. Highsmith's America, Library of Congress, Prints and Photographs Division, LC-DIG-highsm-04758; p. 40b: Library of Congress, Prints and Photographs Division, LC-USZC4-9545; p. 40c: Courtesy of Dave Taylor; p. 41: Library of Congress, Rare Book and Special Collections Division; p. 42: Library of Congress, Prints and Photographs Division, LC-DIG-pga-04067; p. 43a: © iStock.com/Patrice Oehen; p. 43b: Library of Congress, Prints and Photographs Division, LC-USZ62-10122; p. 44a: Library of Congress, Rare Book and Special Collections Division, Alfred Whital Stern Collection of Lincolniana; p. 44b: Library of Congress, Rare Book and Special Collections Division, Alfred Whital Stern Collection of Lincolniana; p. 44c: Courtesy of the Abraham Lincoln Presidential Library and Museum; p. 45a: Library of Congress, Prints and Photographs Division, LC-DIG-ppmsca-23855; p. 45b: Library of Congress, Prints and Photographs Division, LC-DIG-stereo-1s01769; p. 46: Photo © Maxwell McKenzie; p. 47: Photo © Maxwell McKenzie